S0-FNS-624

THE READER'S DOGJEST

CARTOONS AND JOKES FOR CANINE-LOVING FOLKS You'll *WOOF* With Laughter

by Joel Rothman

Published by:
Humor House
Flat 1
12 Ornan Road
Belsize Park
London, NW3 4PX
England

Phone: (44) 207-431-0873
Email: joelrothman@btconnect.com

©Copyright 2006 by Joel Rothman

ISBN: 978-1-930596-51-0

All rights reserved. No part of this book may be reproduced or transmitted in any form or by any means (electronic or mechanical, including photocopy, recording, or any information retrieval system) without the written permission of the publisher.

Distributed by:
The Guest Cottage, Inc
8821 Hwy 47
P.O. Box 848
Woodruff, WI 54568

Phone: 800-333-8122
        715-358-5195
Fax: 715-358-9456
Email: nancytheguestcottage.com

**For Katy,
and in memory
of Fliky
who never met a man
he didn't lick.**

Walking by a pet shop can make some people very emotional. You hear the scratching against the window, the whimpering, the barking, the pleading eyes —— and that's just the owner!

My wife and I decided we wanted to hear the pitter patter of little feet, so we bought a dog. We figured it's cheaper than a baby, and you get more feet.

Dog —— the only true friend you can buy for money.

I'm glad you decided to buy this one —— he's very well-mannered!

I know the pet shop owner said to treat him well — but you don't have to treat him **that** well!

Perhaps it's only a coincidence, but man's best friend can't talk.

If you don't get off
I won't let you watch
the dog food commercial.

Buy *Woof,* the pet food that dogs ask for by name.

Have you heard about the new best-selling book from Vietnam? It's entitled, HOW TO WOK YOUR DOG.

What do they call a Vietnamese family who own a pet dog? *Vegetarians.*

I once ate in a Vietnamese restaurant. The waiter asked me if I wanted my main dish depawed!

In America a dog is for Christmas. In Vietnam a dog is for breakfast, lunch, or supper.

He's a cross —
    half cocker
    half fleas!

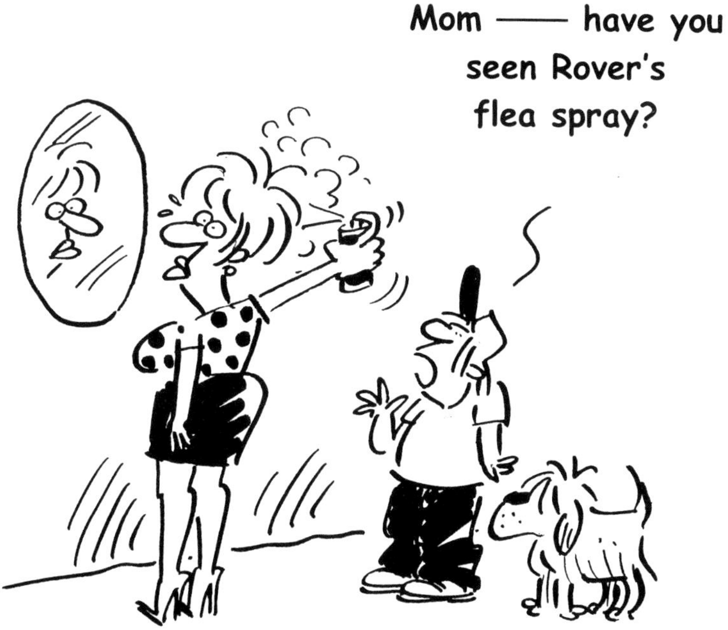
Mom —— have you
seen Rover's
flea spray?

Dogs display
reluctance and wrath
when you try
to give them a bath.

Ogden Nash

This is ridiculous —
why do I have to get in
the tub every time you
decide to wash him?

Doghouse —— a mutt hut.

Drink this water, Tut —— it's very hot today!

He's a great watchdog!
He just sat there and watched the whole thing!

Anyone can teach a dog to fetch a stick, so I decided to teach him to steal.

No matter how worthless a man is, there's always a dog to love him.

The best prayer I ever heard was, "Dear Lord, please make me the kind of person my dog thinks I am."

The canine national anthem: "My Country Tis a Tree."

Misery is having the only tree on a block with twelve dogs.

I took my family on a trip to see the giant redwoods. When we arrived, my dog looked at the trees and nearly had a heart attack.

It's said the fastest dogs live in Siberia —— the trees are so far apart.

Scientists tell us the fastest animal on earth, with a top speed of 100 feet per second, is a dog that's been dropped from a helicopter.

I took my sick dog to a vet. The vet shot him —— it was a Vietnam vet.

Come on champ —— don't be frightened.

A theatrical agent received a call. "Hello," said the voice on the other end. "I need a job —— I can sing, dance and juggle."
"So can dozens of other acts and they're all out of work," snapped the agent.
"I can also play piano and violin, walk a tightrope and recite *Paradice Lost* backwards."
"So can loads of other people —— don't waste my time."
"Wait a minute —— don't hang up —— there's one other thing —— I'm a *dog!*"

I've heard that dogs can talk —— it's untrue. If any dog tells you he can talk, he's lying.

You're a talking dog —— that's great! I can get you a job in the circus . . .

EMPLOYMENT AGENCY

. . . but I'm a plumber!

A man bought a greyhound and taught him to chase rabbits. To his amazement the dog chased a rabbit right across a stream. But instead of swimming across the water the dog just ran across the surface. The astonished owner invited a friend to watch the miracle.
"Well —— what do you think of my dog?" he asked.
The friend said without hesitation, "It's incredible —— I've never before seen a dog that doesn't know how to swim!"

What do you mean
you love me ——
you can't even see
what I look like!

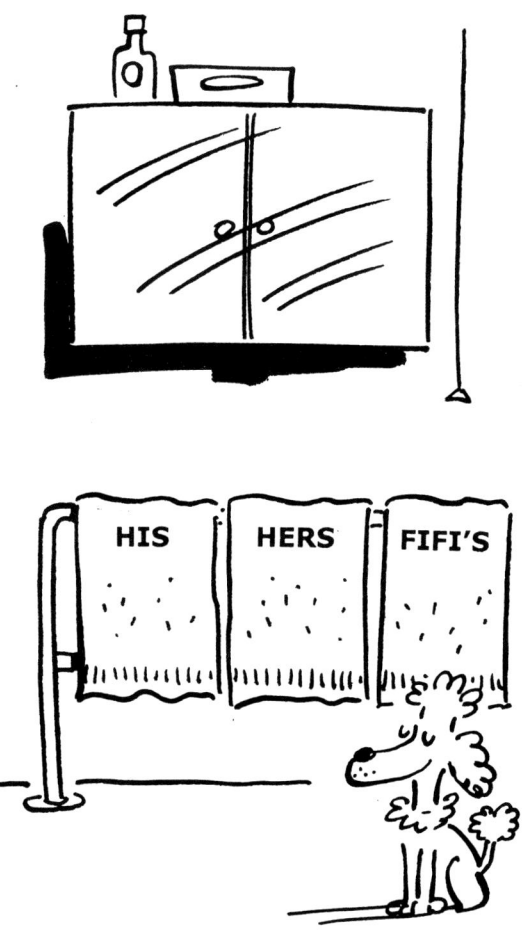

Every morning for seventeen years Ben woke up at six-thirty in the morning and took his dog, Ginger, for a walk. Suddenly Ginger died, and Ben was very distressed. The next morning he woke up at the usual time, stared thoughtfully at the ceiling for a few minutes, then nudged his wife. "Martha," he asked, "you wanna go for a walk?"

Why can't you take him out for a walk like other people?

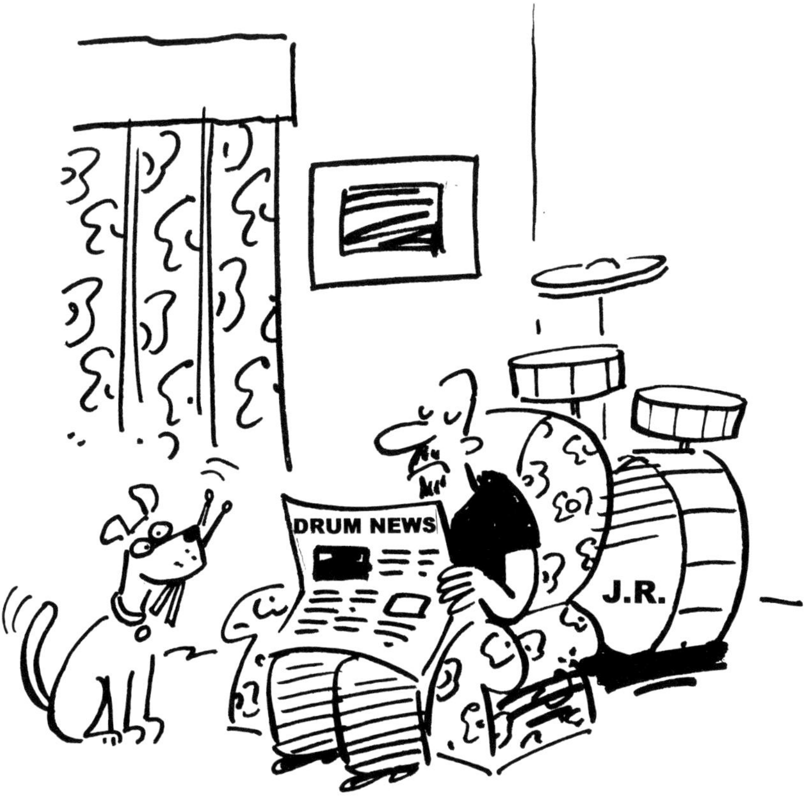
DRUM NEWS
J.R.

Chihuahua —— a bonsai doberman pinscher.

A man with a small chihuahua wanted to go to a restaurant, despite the sign that said *NO DOGS.* So the man put on a pair of dark glasses and tried to walk into the restaurant with his dog. The doorman stopped him and said, "Sorry, no dogs allowed."
"But I'm blind, and this is my new guide dog."
"A chihuahua is a guide dog?" said the doorman in disbelief. "Are you kidding?"
"A chihuahua?" repeated the man, "you mean to say they gave me a chihuahua?"

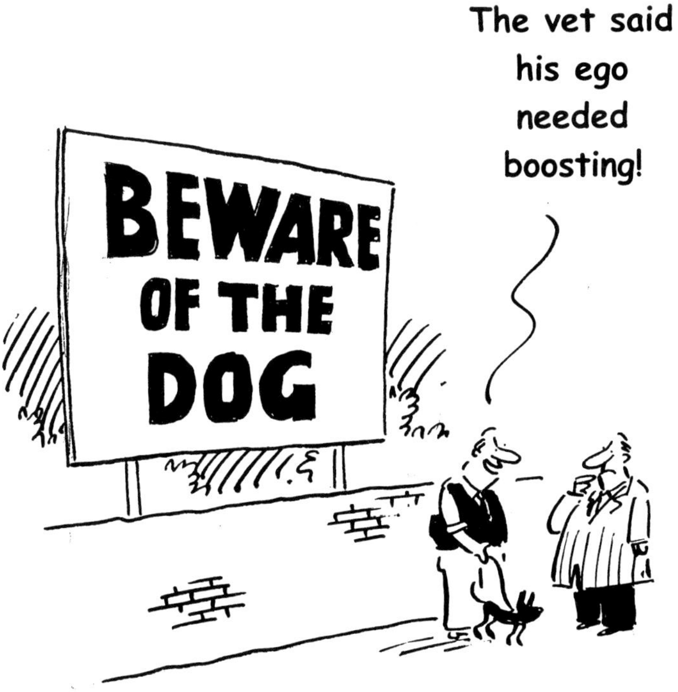
The vet said his ego needed boosting!
BEWARE OF THE DOG

When I asked the woman why she had two seeing eye dogs she told me, "One is for reading."

A blind man walks into a bar, grabs his dog by the hind legs and swings him around in a circle. The bartender asks, "Hey, buddy —— what are you doing?"
"Don't mind me," answers the blind man. "I'm just looking around."

"Why don't blind people go skydiving?"
"It scares the shit out of the dogs!"

Okay, Rex —— bark twice when I'm near the ball.

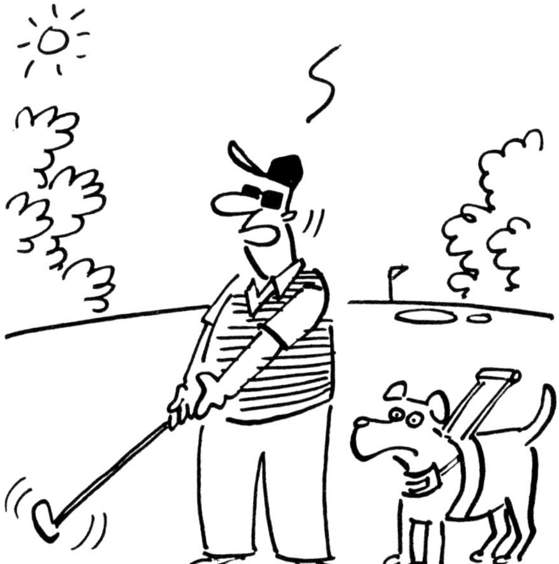

Dog catcher —— a man with a seeing-dog-eye.

It was during the days of prohibition and the railroad station in Louisville was packed with people on their way to a baseball game. Several federal agents were assigned to the area which was notorious for making moonshine. One of the agents noticed that a small man held something under his jacket from which drops were falling. The suspicious agent walked over to the man, put a finger out under one of the drops, and tasted it.
"Whiskey?" he asked.
"Nope," answered the man. "Puppy."

Bertha —— we haven't seen each other in years. Where's that cute little puppy you used to own?

You remember my dog Spot —
well, I accidentally poured spot
remover on him and now he's
disppeared!

The food you served
me is fit for a prince —
'Here Prince, here boy.'

My dog is worried about the high price of dog food — it's now gone up to 99¢ a can, and that's $6.93 in dog money!

Great Dane Puppy —— a dog that has the house broken before it's housebroken!

I once got a Pit Bull as a puppy —— in no time it was eating out of my leg. They say that training can be difficult, but it's not true —— in just a few days I was doing whatever he wanted. But I'll never own a Pit Bull again —— you get it as a puppy, feed it, walk it, train it, take it to the vet when it's sick, give it all the love you've got, then ten years later —— it tries to rip your throat out!

Kiss him on the nose or he'll think you don't like him!

If a dog barks at you while its tail is wagging, how do you know which end to believe?

**I warned you not
to tease that chihuahua.**

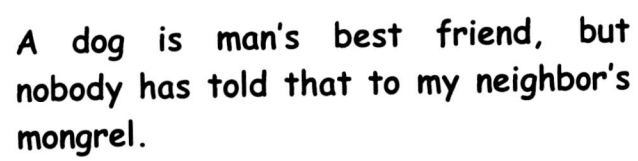

A dog is man's best friend, but nobody has told that to my neighbor's mongrel.

If H_2O is on the inside of a fire hydrant, is K_9P on the outside?

Mrs. Windsor wanted to go on a vacation, but she didn't know what to do with her prize schnauzer. She decided to write to a hotel asking if dogs were allowed, and received the following reply:

Dear Mrs. Windsor,
   I have been managing hotels for almost thirty years, and I have never had to throw out a dog for behaving badly. No dog has ever tried to write a bad check. They never smoke in bed, and not one has ever tried to get away with a single towel. Of course your dog may stay at our establishment.

Sincerely,
The Manager

P.S. And if he vouches for you, you're welcome too.

My dog keeps barking at the front door —— he doesn't want to go out —— he wants *me* to leave!

A playwright returned home only to find that his dog had chewed up three of his unpublished manuscripts.

"Being a dog is not good enough for you," he yelled, "now you have to turn critic!"

Last week I taught my dog how to beg —— so far he's brought me home $24.37.

How humiliating —— personally I would rather borrow or steal!

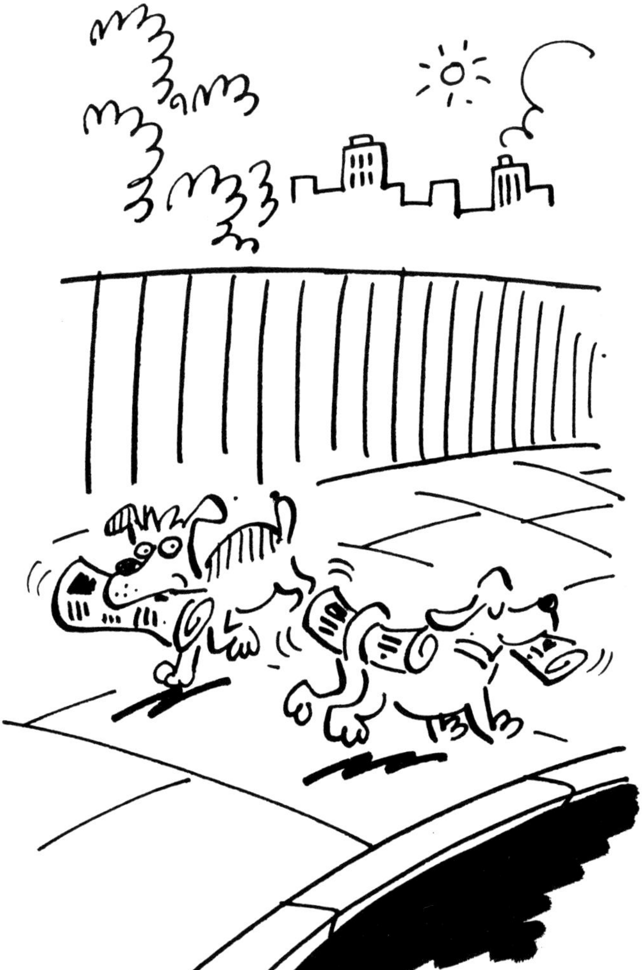

A giant jet passenger plane took off as a man with a sniffer dog roamed the aisles. All of a sudden the dog stopped next to one of the passengers and defecated all over the floor.

"My god, isn't he trained not to do that?" asked the stewardess.

"He is," answered the handler, "but I think he smells a bomb!"

Look at that —
a pay toilet!

My dog must have an exceptionally cold nose —— when he walks into a room all the other dogs quickly sit down.

The beauty of this dog is that you don't have to keep taking it for a walk!

Can you cure him, doc?
The wind-up
mechanism seems
to be stuck!

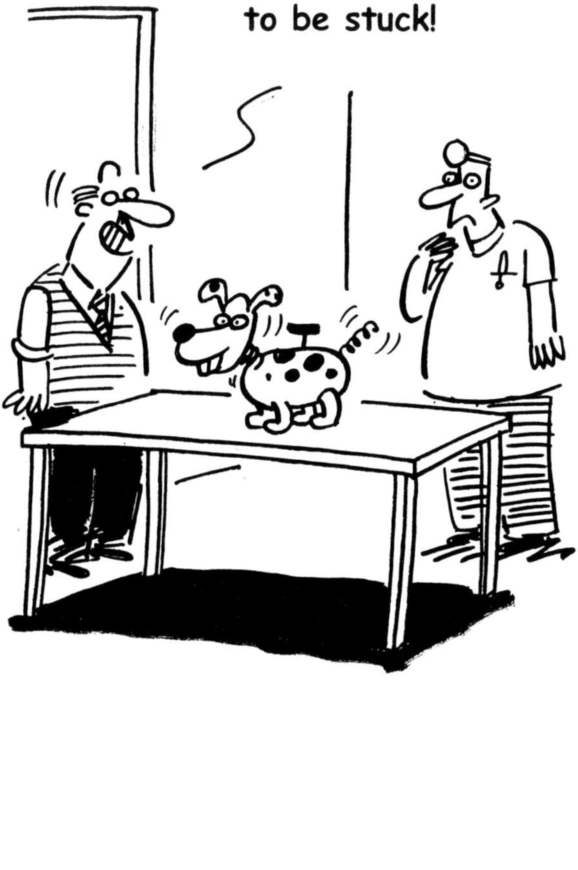

Thanks —— I would have preferred a beef steak but the St. Bernard was delicious!

I knew of one St. Bernard that ran away and was never heard from again. Apparently he discovered what was in the keg.

The winning dog at Crufts was a real show-*arf*.

A young woman was terribly fond of her pet airedale, but the dog darted into the street one day and was killed by a passing motorist. Her husband came home from work and found her crying hysterically.
"Tell me what happened?"
"Our Ruby was run over and now she's dead," sobbed the wife.
The husband tried to comfort her.
"Now, now," he said, "calm down and I'll buy you another dog."
"Another dog!" screamed the wife. "Why, if you realized how much I adored Ruby, you'd buy me a fur coat!"

If you and your husband have both been so unhappy, why didn't you get divorced?
We've stayed together for the sake of the dog.
SAUNA

Some things don't make sense —— for instance, I'm married and we own a beautiful female poodle. Every evening when I come home from work that poodle jumps all over me and wags her tail like crazy. It's my wife who barks at me!

Is it really necessary to send a Christmas card from Rover to Mrs. Wilson's dog?

I had to get rid of
my husband — my
dog was allergic.

A man likes to have a dog worship him
— a woman likes to have a dog to
worship.

. . . then I told the wife, either the dog goes or I go!

Don't you think it's time you started taking the dog for a proper walk?

Why can't you
walk her in the
park like other
dog owners?

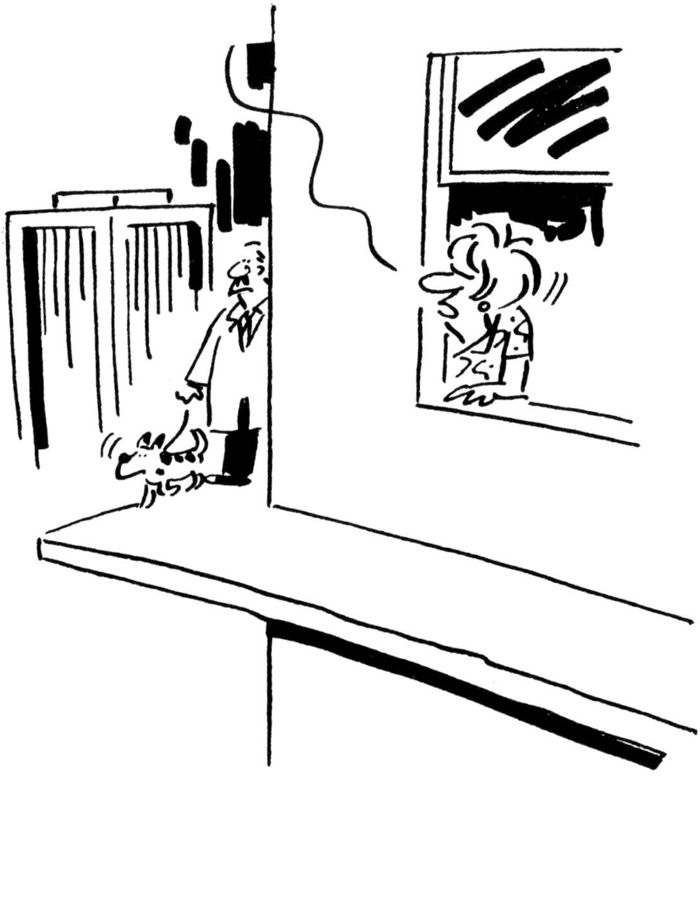

If a dog's prayers were answered would it rain bones?

This is ridiculous ——
why can't she remember
where she buried them?

er . . . I hope you're not wearing an expensive pair of stockings, Jean!

Our new dog has an unusual way to let us know he's hungry!

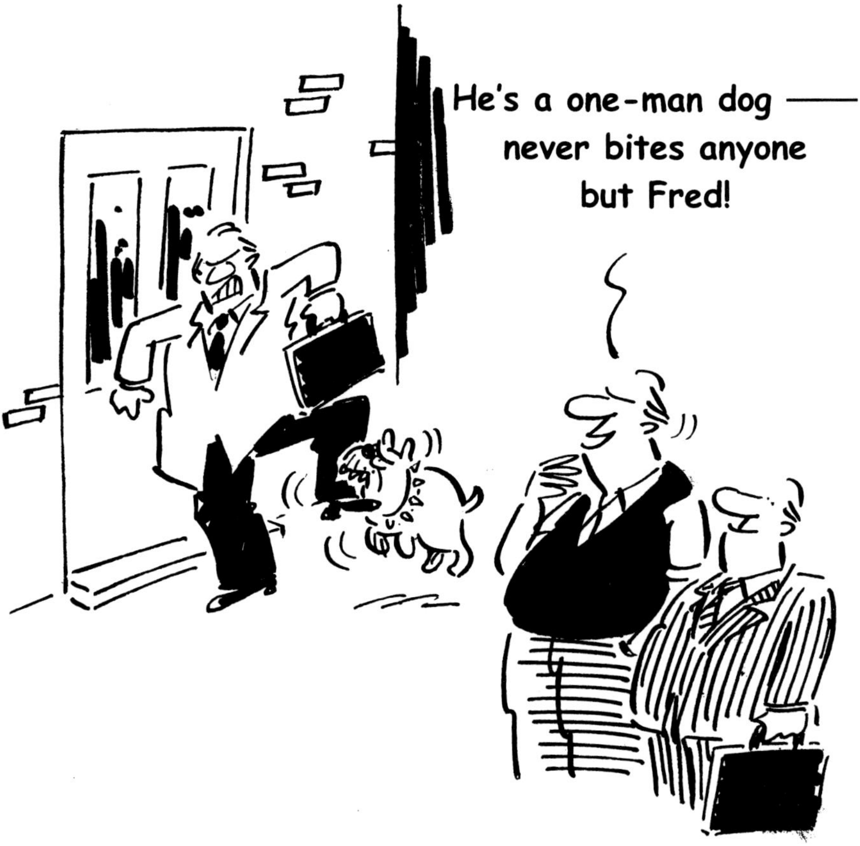
He's a one-man dog —
never bites anyone
but Fred!

A mad dog bit a
tax inspector —
after being given an
injection and treated
for shock the dog was
allowed to go home . . .

When I said cough
I wasn't talking
to your dog!

"I reckon he's swallowed someone's dog!"

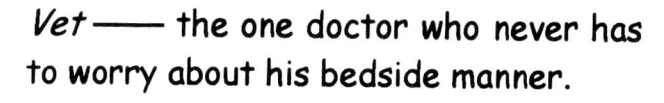

Vet —— the one doctor who never has to worry about his bedside manner.

Ivan's teacher asked, "How was your weekend?"

"Horrible —— a car hit my dog in the ass."

"Rectum," said the teacher. "Say rectum."

"Rectum?" replied Ivan. "Why it damn near killed him!"

A young girl ran to tell her mother she found a dead dog by the side of the road.

"How do you know it's dead?" asked the mother.

"Because I pissed in its ear and it didn't move," came the reply.

"You did what?" asked the shocked mother at her daughter's language.

"You know," explained the young girl, "I leaned over and went *pssst,* and it didn't move."

Why has it taken you so long to bury your dog?
It wouldn't stop moving!
R.I.P. FLIKY

Paddy was a Newfoundland who was accidentally killed by a van during the morning. The owner was distraught and extremely anxious about the way her young son might react when he heard the news. The boy finally returned from school and yelled, "Here Paddy, here boy." The mother had to tell him that Paddy was killed in the morning by a small truck. "Oh," said the boy as he walked to his room, humming as if nothing had happened.
"Robert," called his mother, "I just told you that Paddy was killed." Immediately the boy began to cry, tears streaming from his eyes. "That's strange," said the mother, "when I told you the first time it didn't seem to bother you."
The boy was so choked up he could barely answer. "It's because I thought you said *Daddy*."

After my terrier died
I swore I'd never get
another dog!

Brothers and Sisters,
I bid you beware
Of giving your heart
To a dog to share.

Rudyard Kipling

"I don't like that dachshund," said the little girl. "It's legs are too short."

"What do you mean too short?" replied the pet salesman. "They reach the ground, don't they?"

I want the one with the happy ending!